The Little Book
About Toxic Friends

Zara –
Thank you for your
support! I hope you enjoy
my book! Thank you!

Joyce M. Gilliard

The Little Book About Toxic Friends

How To Recognize A Toxic Relationship

Joyce M. Gilliard

To order additional copies of this book, contact:
Xlibris
1-888-795-4274
www.Xlibris.com
Orders@Xlibris.com
734433

For My Family.

I want to personally thank everyone who believed, supported, and encouraged me. If it wasn't for my family and friends, I would have possibly waited to pursue my dreams as an author. I know that life has thrown many curves, but you have continuously showed me support through the years. I would like to thank Tracy G. for being my biggest supporter for over twenty-five years. Jereme G., Kenee' G., and Tracy Jr.—thank you for your unconditional love, even during the times when I wasn't myself. I want to thank my mom and my entire family, who encouraged me to write this book. I would like to thank my friends for the memories and experiences that encouraged growth, so I could be a better person. Thank you, Candace G., Karen K., and AnTonyia V., for pushing me to write, even when I felt like I didn't have it in me.

Introduction

How many of you have a friend whom you thought would be your friend to the end? It may have been a childhood friend, high school buddy, or even a college roommate. You were always together. You couldn't see life without this person. You would have children, spouses, the big house, the dog, go on vacation, and do everything together. He or she knew secrets. You would do mischievous, sometimes risky things with this person that you wouldn't do with anyone else. One word, one glance, was enough to set you both convulsing in laughter.

You were right about how good the friendship was, but wrong about forever. Instead, you have a friend who causes you so much pain and heartache. You try to hold onto a relationship long past the stage when it was good. You don't realize you are in what has become an unhealthy relationship, although the signs are there. The signs are always there. I want to help you. I am not a psychiatrist, psychologist, or a doctor. None of the information is based on scientific studies. I am only recounting my experiences with friends whom I consider toxic to me and my well-being. Some of the stories are for entertainment, to enhance reading enjoyment. No one's real name is used in this book. Even though some situations may have similarities to yours, it is not about you. In this book, I will give you the signs and share experiences that will help you determine whether your relationship is "toxic." You will also evaluate yourself to see if you are the toxic friend.

Chapter 1

Many friendships begin in the early years. Some start in your first year at school, while others blossom later in life. Friendships back in the day were always easy to make. Those were the days of interaction, before the Internet. We used to play games outside—such as hide-and-seek, catch and kickball, and running to see who was the fastest. Children would make up games to play until the streetlights came on. We would roller-skate in the streets, skateboard, dance, and even play board games.

When you moved into a new neighborhood, you would always look out the window to see if there were other kids in the neighborhood. I remember just walking up and down the street, displaying myself so other kids could see me and come outside to play. It was easy to make friends. All you had to do was go outside with a Barbie doll, basketball, or football. It always lured other kids out of their houses. Those were the days. I don't think it's wise to do that now. Nobody would come out, and they'd think you are weird.

As a child, you never knew if a friendship was a good one for you. Only your parents could see right through people. They would warn you and tell you that you couldn't be friends with someone. Of course, as a kid, you usually wouldn't listen. You would sneak out to play with your "banned" friend.

In your teen years, you would go through friends quickly. Every day, you would have a new friend. Drama always seemed to find its way into your relationship. Instead of focusing on schoolwork, you focused more on your social life. Being popular seemed to be every teenager's priority in school. Instead of lasting friendships, you acquired toxic ones. Parents always could distinguish between the real friends and the toxic ones. Sometimes you saw the signs that your mother always told you about, but you didn't care because parents were lame and didn't know anything.

As you matured and became an adult, you would try to always seek the good in people. You really didn't believe people could be toxic, until a repetition of behaviors and attitudes caused you heartache.

What is *toxic*? *Toxic* is something that is not good for you. If anything that is done to you by your friend causes stress, hair loss, weight loss, weight gain, anxiety, depression, anger, and other health issues, it is toxic. If your friend makes you feel like hurting somebody, then you are in a toxic relationship.

There are many types of toxic friends. I listed a few types that you may be familiar with and others that you probably haven't been subjected to yet.

1. Friends who never seem happy for you.
2. Friends who don't want you to succeed.
3. Friends who are never there for you.
4. Friends who always want what you have.
5. Friends who hurt you physically or emotionally.
6. Friends who talk about you negatively to others.
7. Friends who tell all of your business.
8. Friends who degrade you.
9. Friends who never uplift you.
10. Friends who are jealous and envious of you.
11. Friends who are pathological liars.
12. Friends who are miserable and want you to be the same.
13. Fake friends.

There you have it, my thirteen varieties of a toxic friend. I will go in-depth about each one and give examples in the next few chapters. What I am saying may be hilarious; you may not even take me seriously. I am writing based on my experiences from situations that I have been through or stories that others have shared with me. The names that are used are not the actual persons', so please don't think I am talking about you. Many of my experiences have been with women friends.

If the story that I am sharing is similar to something that you are going through, then look at it as confirmation that you are in a toxic relationship. I hope that it helps you recognize your toxic friendship. It may even help determine if you are that toxic friend.

I am happy for you. When you have a friend, you always feel that you should be happy for each other, right? In a perfect world, yes—but we all know this is not the case. We should always be happy for each other and celebrate each other's success. But sometimes friends just can't *handle the process of the elevation to success.* I want to clarify what I mean by the previous sentence. To be successful, we all start from the bottom before we make it to the top. If you have close friends who are there with you in the beginning, they watch your growth and the steps you have taken to become successful. Your friend encourages you and often helps you along the way, but in many cases, some friends can't handle it. During that process, they can't show happiness because they know what the likely outcome will be: success. I have friends like this, and I know you probably do too. I could give many examples from my life, but I will give an example that was shared with me.

You and your friend both have the same aspiration: to become successful authors. Both of you attend the same school. You struggle the entire year with writing assignments, while your friend aces through them. She would give you encouraging words and tell you that you will get better. As long as you were getting lower grades than your friend, everything was fine.

You work really hard, and eventually your grades exceed your expectations. Your GPA is a 4.0 while your friend's GPA is a 3.0. You are excited that you made a 4.0, especially after struggling for so long. You tell your friend. You jump up and down with excitement and share it with your friend. She jumps along with you (*fake friend*), but in her heart, she is upset because you got the 4.0 and she didn't. You don't even realize that your GPA bothered your friend. Every time you would get your grades, they were better than you friend's. You start realizing that she is not sincerely happy for you as you initially thought, based on her responses, body language, and facial expressions. You stop sharing your achievements because you don't want your friend to be upset (*jealous friend*).

Your friend starts to seem uninterested in any exciting news and stops listening to you. She changes the subject or even walks away, as if she were busy and not able to listen. She may even think that you are bragging. It's not bragging when you want to share your accomplishments with your friend. You share it so that you both can celebrate. Only your friend knew and understood your struggle. It is only natural that you would assume that your friend would be happy for you.

Once you start noticing the change in your friend, you start to question her and ask if she is okay. Some friends, who can be honest, may admit their envy and apologize for it. That's not the kind of friend I'm talking about. I am referring to the kind who says "everything is fine" or "I am happy for you," but feels otherwise. The tone in their voice, body language, and the look in their eyes lets you know right away that there is a problem. The signs are prevalent, but you just don't want to accept them. After all, this is your friend, your road dog. You expect your road dog to be happy for you, right?

Reality finally sets in, and you realize that they are not. They are upset because you are doing an exceptional job and have a 4.0 GPA. Why would your friend not be happy for you? If you have been friends for many years, happiness should go with the territory.

This is toxic. Holding things inside is not healthy, whether it is positive or negative. It can lead to serious health conditions such as depression and anxiety.

Sometimes you question yourself and wonder if you did something wrong. Did you rub it in your friend's face? Did you tell your friend so that they could be jealous? You only shared your excitement and happiness with your friend, who happens to not be happy for you. If you are that type of person who is never happy for your friend, then you need to evaluate yourself, because you may be toxic. Be wary of toxic friends. The signs aren't always visible, but if you pay close attention, they will eventually reveal their true selves.

When your friend isn't truly happy for you, it can lead into a lifetime full of deceit, heartache, and turmoil.

A friend who is not happy for you is a *hater*. A hater can't stand to see you succeed and will do or say anything negative to discourage you. A hater will shrug their nose at you and say that *you think you are all that.* When someone tells you that, take it as a compliment and know that they are the ones who think that about you. Keep your haters happy by continuously striving to be successful. A hater will try to break you down physically, mentally, and emotionally. A hater will scroll down your timeline, read your status, watch what you post, and won't like what you post. Some friends will think that your posts are about them, when it doesn't have anything to do with them. Many people thrive on getting "likes" and get upset if you don't "like" their status. People need to remember that getting a "like" on social media doesn't define who you are. It really doesn't matter if they like it, because social media can be very deceiving. Many people use it as a platform to fabricate lies anyway.

If you share everything you do on social media, it opens the door for positive and negative comments. A hater will always have something negative to say. Instead of complimenting you, a hater will attempt to discredit you and your success. A friend who is a hater can be very deceiving.

Chapter 2

I want to see you succeed. Everyone wants to succeed, right? Most friends, the non-toxic ones, do want you to succeed, while the toxic ones are really saying *I don't want you to succeed or do better than me.* I know it seems harsh, but it's true. As I said previously, some friends can't handle *the process of the elevation to success.* I have a story to tell you about two friends.

Miscelle and Roxanne have been friends for over twenty years. They were childhood friends. Roxanne was four years older than Miscelle. These friends were both hairstylists. The two friends met in beauty school and became lifelong friends. Miscelle always struggled and did things on her own, while Roxanne had her family to support her. Roxanne always would tell Miscelle that she was opening up her own hair salon. Miscelle wanted to also, but she never dreamed that she would. She always knew that Roxanne would open her salon up, and she would work as her assistant. It was all set up for Roxanne by her family. The problem was that Roxanne was a procrastinator. She was the type of person who would always say what she wanted to do, but she never did what she always said. Miscelle, on the other hand, would dream it; she would want to do things but didn't have the resources to live out her dreams or desires.

The two friends graduated from beauty school at the same time. Roxanne immediately started working in a multicultural salon to build a client base, while Miscelle moved away with her new family, in which she had to start over. While the two friends were separated, Roxanne continued to tell Miscelle that she was opening a salon. Miscelle worked in several salons on commission and became a booth renter once she established her clientele.

One day, Miscelle woke up and decided that she was going to step out in faith and open a salon. She had saved some money, established her client base, and felt like the timing was right. She told Roxanne what her plans were. Roxanne didn't believe Miscelle, and she didn't encourage her to open up the salon either. Roxanne knew that she always wanted to open up a salon for many years, but procrastinated. She appeared to be happy that Miscelle was doing this, but had no idea that it was going to happen right away. In her mind, she was thinking that it would be a year or so before Miscelle would do it. It would give her time to move fast, to open her salon first. It didn't. Miscelle opened her salon within two weeks from the time that she had originally told her. Roxanne was not happy for her. Roxanne never called Miscelle or visited to help her celebrate the opening of her salon. Miscelle's salon became one of the most successful salons in New York.

You see, sometimes it is difficult for some friends to celebrate your success—if they are not successful. Instead of helping you, lifting you up, and encouraging you, they choose to not engage in any activity that would promote your success. I know that it is hard to accept that a friend would be uncaring. A true friend would celebrate with you. A friend could express to you all day that they were happy for you.

Pay attention to their actions. Have you ever been so happy to share things with your friend, couldn't wait until they were available to talk, and once you reach them, they acted as if you were crazy and didn't share the same enthusiasm? Isn't that the worst feeling? You end up bringing the excitement down a notch because of their response. Have you ever heard of the saying "Actions speak louder than words"? There is truth to that saying. Rely on the things that your friend does, and not on what they say. Relying on words will hurt you every time. You start to expect things because of what they said.

You always get hurt when you expect things. Miscelle expected that because Roxanne was her friend, she would celebrate her success. If Roxanne had opened up her salon first, she may have been a little more accepting of Miscelle's salon. A friendship shouldn't be like this. Roxanne was jealous and a hater.

When you realize that your friend does not want to see you succeed, you start questioning yourself and wondering what you did that would warrant this. It starts to weigh on your mind and becomes a distraction for you so you can't focus on the success of your business. This is a toxic relationship. You have a toxic friend. It is time to evaluate your friendship. If your friend can't celebrate your success, then he or she is not your friend. I have experienced this type of friend many times. After the first few times, you would think that I would learn and discern quickly. I learned the hard way when it came to friends.

Sometimes a friend may not want you to be successful but would want to enjoy the benefits of your success. How many of you know someone like that? They are the ones who don't contribute to your success; but as soon as an event comes up where they can dress up and show off, they are right there smiling in your face, ready to receive the benefits (*fake friends*).

Why don't friends understand that if you succeed, they succeed? Does anyone understand that concept? Instead of not wanting you to succeed and hating on you because of your success, they should be supportive. No one truly wants to be successful without sharing it with their friend, or bringing their friend along every step of the way.

People don't see the big picture. If your friend does not want to see you succeed, then you have a toxic friend. This type of friend will do things to hold you back. It is the "crab in the barrel" mentality.

Have you heard of this saying before? Have you ever had blue crabs? When you put the crabs in the water, the crabs try to climb out. While they try to climb out, the other crabs keep pulling at each other so they can all go in the water. The crabs struggle to get out, but the others won't let it happen. Eventually, they all suffer together and none of the crabs escape. A toxic friend will do this to you. They will keep pulling you back so that you won't succeed.

Some friends may already be successful, and you may have contributed to their success. I recall a situation when a friend of mine started a business. She had several business ventures going at one time. When she needed advice or assistance with any of her businesses, I was there to help. I canceled events that I had going on, just to help her. I wasn't on her payroll and did not get paid. I got many promises though. She always promised to bring me up with her, to be a part of her team. As her business started to prosper, I was very excited for her. I watched her grow an empire from the ground up, with the help of others. She started to become distant after her success. I remember reaching out to her for help with a few of my business ventures, and I was taken aback by her response. She didn't have the time to help—and if she did, it would be for a substantial fee.

Don't get me wrong; I will pay for what I need. But for someone whom I did not charge a fee to for several years, to help her business grow—to suggest that she would help me for a fee really took me by surprise. She burned many bridges to be successful and did not come through with any of her promises. People who forget who helped them succeed and won't give back and reciprocate the same are selfish. They may not even realize their selfish ways. In their minds, they do all they can to help others, and they applaud themselves for it. I won't say they are toxic, but they can make the situation toxic because of the resentment one can feel because they were used for free services, but when help is needed on their behalf, it was done for a fee. It will make a person think back to the many days and nights spent with no pay to help. They will think of all the physical labor and the emotional roller coasters they endured to help in the success.

On the flip side, many people also think because you are friends, they don't have to pay for services. If your friend has a business, the way you can support them is by not assuming that if they provide you services, it's for free. It took time, money, resources, and investments for the business to start; and it will take money and customers to survive. If your friend didn't charge services for all her friends, then how would she make money? It's different if you both have a mutual agreement in which you decide to use the barter system. It is ultimately up to your friend, the business owner. Many friendships have become toxic because of making assumptions. Having conversations in the beginning will help ensure the relationship does not become toxic.

We are focused on friends, but sometimes people in your family are toxic. I know this may strike a nerve with some, but it's true. If it does strike a nerve, then you must be the toxic family member. Some family members don't want to see you succeed. They will do the same things a toxic friend does. The difference between a toxic family member and a toxic friend is that you can get rid of that toxic friend. Family is blood. Once you figure out that your family member is toxic, all you need to do is distance yourself from them, because you can't get rid of them.

Toxic family members will keep drama going. They are constantly causing confusion and problems. They are always in your business, and instead of giving you advice to help you, they will smile in your face and talk about your situation to other family members. Some family members will act like they are happy for your success, but they are happier if you fail. They won't support you in your endeavors, but they will brag about them to others so they can look good. I am not saying that all family members are like this. Many family members are loving, caring, and supportive. I am speaking about the ones who aren't.

Chapter 3

I want what you have. Have you ever had that friend who would get everything that you have, or try to get one up on you, so that it would be better than yours? Have you ever had that friend who would go out with your boyfriend right after you break up? Have you had that friend who took your man? Have you had that friend who wants your life rather than their own? Have you had that friend who always seems to compete with you? If you can answer yes to any of those questions, then you have a toxic friendship.

I was watching a TV show one night about girlfriends. One of the friends (host) invited the other two over for dinner. After a night of drinking, the hostess started to verbally abuse the other two friends. During her rant, she told her friend that her man kept her on a leash, and in the next breath, she said that she wanted *her life*. The friend was shocked that she said this to her. It was very apparent that the host was jealous of the relationship that her friend had with her man. The two were always together. If being kept on a leash was what she saw instead of two people that loved each other's company, then that was the host's problem. She hated seeing the two of them together, and because she was drunk, she was able to verbalize her true feelings.

Of course, the friend told her that she couldn't have her life and she needed to work on having her own. There are so many friends out there who want what you have. In this situation, the host was feeling this way for a long time, while the friend had no clue. I am sure the signs were there. They say that when you are drinking, you speak the truth. If alcohol wasn't involved, would the friend ever know that her friend wanted her life? Or would she have kept thinking that all was well? I am not talking about when a person has dreams to be like someone—maybe a mentor, a celebrity, or someone who has impacted their lives—but to want someone's life and not your own may be a bit much, especially if you don't like a person because their life is, in their eyes, better than yours.

When a woman has a best friend, they sometimes share too much information. Some things we just have to keep to ourselves. You can't share all your dreams with your friend and tell them about your relationships or desires. This is one mistake that is made often. Most of the time, you can be the one who has a significant other, while your friend, on the other hand, is single. It's always the single friend who will give you negative advice. Usually, the negative advice comes because they want what you have or want to destroy what you have because of their unhappiness. Misery loves company.

I can remember telling my friend my dreams and aspirations. I wanted a nice car, a nice home, a husband,

and a good job. I have a story to share to show you the lengths a friend would go to have what you have.

I worked at a fast-food restaurant, just to make ends meet. I needed a car badly. My friend had a luxury car. She would get a new car every few years. I would walk, catch a bus, or hitch a ride to get to work. I expressed to my friend that my dream car at the time was an Explorer SUV. I talked about the Explorer all the time.

One day, after I got home from work, my friend came by my home excited. She said that she had something to show me. I was excited because she was excited, so I couldn't wait to see what it was. She took me outside, and there it was. She bought a brand-new Explorer. My eyes got wide with excitement because I honestly thought it was for me! I started to hug her and ask questions about how she was able to get me the Explorer. She laughed and said that I was silly. I was confused at her statement. She told me that it was her truck! She traded her luxury vehicle in for the Explorer.

I couldn't believe it. Why would a person trade in a luxury vehicle for an Explorer? She never said that she wanted to get that type of vehicle. Maybe she didn't tell me that she wanted an Explorer because she would be sharing too much information. I didn't know what to feel. She laughed and said that she got her truck first, and then she wanted us to take photos together next to the truck!

I thought that was so cruel. It was amusing to her. She wanted me to see that she could get whatever she wanted, and I had to work hard for it. She also just wanted to rub it in my face and see how I would react. Was it in my mind that she was doing this to me deliberately? Was I not happy for my friend? Was I the *toxic friend* for not truly being happy for her?

I probably was, because I really wasn't happy for her. I was pissed off because I had been talking about this SUV for years. I thought it was a sick joke how she presented the SUV to me. Not only did my friend get the truck of my dreams, but she took my man too!

My friend was always the one I would go shopping with. I remember one day, a very long time ago, we went shopping. We met a group of handsome doctors who were on their lunch break. I was the shy one, while my friend was outgoing. I showed her the doctor who caught my attention. He was short, stout, and not her type. The other doctor was very tall and her type. The doctors gave her their phone numbers. Instead of giving me the telephone number of the one that I was interested in, she kept it to herself and started to establish a relationship with him. He wasn't her type at all, but because I was interested, she decided to make a move on him. I was so upset that she started to have a relationship with him only because I showed interest.

She always wanted what I had. I was always too trusting with her. I became afraid to share anything with her, because of the fear that she would try to take it from me. I began to hide things from her. I only shared things with her that she could not destroy or take.

Of course, the relationship my friend had with the doctor didn't last two months. I finally met someone. We were together for a year but had many ups and downs. Every time we had a problem, I would go run and tell my friend. She would say things like "He doesn't want you," "He is cheating on you," "He is not a good man," or "Girl, you need to leave him." She never said anything positive to me about my relationship.

My man finally got tired of me running to my friend, so we broke up. That wasn't the main reason, but it was one of them. After we broke up, guess who had a shoulder for him to cry on? Yes, my girlfriend did. She didn't lend her shoulder to me, she lent it to him. Of course, she seduced him into believing that she was the woman he needed. I am happy that the relationship ended anyway, because I married a wonderful man.

How many of you have a friend who will steal your man? So many friends will listen to you talk about your man, and they will give you bogus advice about your relationship when, all along, they wish they had *what you have.* This is a toxic friendship. If your friend makes you feel like you want to beat them down, then it is a toxic relationship. Leave the friendship before you stoop that low in any relationship.

Remember, never share all your intimate thoughts, dreams, goals, and anything about your man—whether it's positive or negative—with your friend. Your friend is only waiting for the opportunity to step in and *take what you have.*

Chapter 4

Have you ever had a friend who is never there for you? Have you had that friend who only thinks of themselves? Have you ever been in a conversation with a friend and the conversation is one-sided? Your friend is always talking and never listening? I know many of you have experienced it at one point with a toxic friend. Have you ever called your friend, and they seem disinterested in what you have to say? They may be on the phone with you but distracted or even talking to someone else in the background, while you are trying to hold a conversation with them. There are many pauses in the conversation because you are waiting for them to give you their attention. All of a sudden, you have their attention, and then they change the subject to something about them. The conversation always changes or flips to what they want to talk about and then you find yourself swept into their self-centered ways.

If you have a friend like this, then it is a toxic relationship. A conversation should go both ways. A person should be willing to give and receive, as you should be able to speak and listen. If you are always giving in the relationship, it can be very draining. A toxic friend will suck your spirit dry. They will take, take, take, and never give. Friends who are draining and are too much work are toxic. These people will leave you with a headache and heartache. I forgot to mention those friends who are always full of drama. They always have drama and you always are there to listen to their drama.

If you are the one who is always listening and never able to speak, this is not healthy. A true friend will let you express yourself, and vice-versa. It should never be a one-sided conversation. A friend like that is usually self-centered. If you have to chase your friend for love, attention, and affection, then they are toxic to you. I feel they want to listen or care, but everything has to be about them. If it isn't about them, then they don't want to listen. Not being able to talk or express yourself can cause problems, and can lead to health issues. Keeping everything inside is never good. It can lead to headaches, sadness, and depression. I know this because I experienced it myself. I am only speaking of my experiences. I have had every type of friend that you can think of!

If you have a friend who has these self-centered traits, then it is impossible for them to always be there for you. This leads me into another type of friend.

I will always be there for you. I know we all expect our friends to always be there for us. This isn't true when you have a toxic friend. A toxic friend will never be there for you. It only seems natural to expect it, but a self-centered friend is always thinking about themselves, and seldom thinks about anyone else. They would expect you to be there for them all the time, but they are never there for you. Sometimes I wonder if it is an inherited trait. It hurts most of us more knowing that your friend isn't there for you, more than any other type of toxic friend. You are always there for them, and will do anything for them within your means. You bend over backward for them and support them as often as you can.

Do you have a friend like that? I know you do. A toxic friend won't celebrate life with you, whether it's good or bad, because life only revolves around them. I know what I said was deep. Let those words resonate with you. *Life only revolves around them.* Stop expecting them to be there for you. Expecting too much is the reason why you are subjected to hurt, pain, and disappointments.

I have a few examples of a friend that wasn't there for me, but I was always there for them. If you can relate to this, then you have a toxic friend.

My friend and I had children who were around the same ages. I invited her to every event, but she always was a no-show. She was always pre-occupied and disinterested in anything I had going on. When her children graduated from school, I was there to celebrate. Every play, soccer game, or event that her children had, I was always there cheering them on and supporting them. When it came time for my children's events, she was always absent. I recall when I was having a birthday celebration. I resided out of state, but was planning my birthday celebration in my hometown. I planned for one year. It was going to be a huge celebration. My friend and I stayed on the telephone daily, discussing the plans for my party during the entire year. A few days before my party, my friend disappeared! I called her countless times, visited her home, left messages and emailed with no responses from her. I was terrified that something bad happened to her. On the day of my party, I tried to remain calm. It was difficult to enjoy myself without knowing what happened to her. I feared the worse. She didn't attend and I didn't speak to her for several weeks. One day, I called her from an unrecognizable telephone number. She answered the call on the first ring! My heart skipped a beat. I didn't know whether to be upset with her or relieved that nothing bad happened to her. I preceded to ask her what happened to her. She thought it was unnecessary to give me an explanation, and she didn't. I didn't understand what was going on with her and why she was ignoring that she did something wrong. I was heartbroken. I searched my heart and mind to seek answers that she would not give me. After years, when I started to assess the friendship, I realized how absent she was from my life, the disappointments and heartache she caused. Even then, I held on to the friendship and still did not let it go. It wasn't until a life-altering event that helped me to understand that you have to release the bad things that happened in your past, so you can move on to receive the blessings in your future.

I was in a horrific accident and was severely injured. I almost died. I was hospitalized for a few days and had to undergo surgery. My friend never visited me at the hospital, never called, and was never there to help me. It really hurt me. Instead of waiting around for my friend to call me, I reached out and left many messages I realized how life is too short to be angry at people or hold grudges because they did you wrong. I wanted to let my friend know that I forgave her a long time ago. I thought that because of our history as friends, we would have reconnected after the trauma that I went through. I had a newfound perspective on life and I wanted to make things right. After several months, I finally got a response. She told me that she was unable to talk and she would call me back later. As of present day, I have not heard from her.

I never knew what happened and I probably will never know. If there were issues in our relationship, I thought that my traumatic experience would have brought us together again. Strangers came to my aid to comfort me. People who were not close to me gave me support. I never thought the people whom I called my friends would be absent during the time that I needed them most. People who were associates or colleagues, helped me more than I could repay. I will forever show gratitude to them and I will always remember the people who were present. I had friends who made promises that they were coming by to help me, but all of the promises were broken. Never believe a promise. No one should ever make promises, because they will always be broken.

Many of those friends felt bad because they didn't do what they said, they didn't call, or visit. I have been disappointed time after time. A person would think that I should have it figured out by now that I have had toxic friendships. You see, when you are in it, you don't think you are. It may take another friend or family member to tell you to pay attention.

I know that you are wondering if I have friends. I do have them. I just have had many toxic ones. In my eyes, and in my heart, I try to see the good in people. The signs were always there to let me know that someone was toxic, but I chose to disregard them. I started to get headaches, experienced skin problems, and sometimes I experienced chest pains. The pains were from a broken heart. It really bothered me that my friend and the others were not there for me, especially through the worst times of my life. We had been friends for over fifteen years. I had over fifteen years of being in a toxic relationship. I have accepted it and moved on. It gave me the tools to write this book.

I will help you. How many of you have that friend that you you always helped out, but never helped you in return? It doesn't matter who you are, you have had that type of friend. You are always giving and they are always taking. It amazes me some friends don't know how to give, because their hands are always open to receive. If you are always the one giving in your friendship and never getting anything back, then you are in a toxic relationship.

A friendship should work both ways. Everyone should benefit from having a friend. You are supposed to help each other. Friction will always occur when the relationship is one-sided. You will start to feel like you are being used for what you can give. You are always giving. If you ask your friend to help you, there is always an excuse why they can't help you. Let go of this friend. The relationship is only providing security for one party, which happens to be that toxic friend. That friend knows that you will always be there for them and will suck all the generosity and kindness out of you. You will end up having nothing left, and you will feel used in the process. Feeling used is always a hurtful thing. It can cause severe heartache and depression. This type of friend is a toxic friend.

Chapter 5

I *will never hurt you*. How many of you always believe that your friend will never hurt you? It just doesn't seem like it's possible, right? Well, think again. You will always get hurt by someone, whether it's your friend or family. A best friend is someone you confide in and share your inner thoughts with. Sometimes you cringe at the thought of them hurting you. Every example that I gave thus far in this book all have one thing in common. Each situation hurts. You are only human. Each one of these traits that your friend has does hurt. That's why your friend is toxic.

If hurt and pain are always associated with your friend, then that friend is toxic. I don't need to give examples because you all have examples of your own. When a friend hurts you, you feel as if it is the end of the world. You are often in disbelief, and you harbor the hurtful feelings and start to feel resentment. This is not healthy. You should never allow anyone to make you feel resentment toward them. If you feel this way, that means it is time to let that friend go. You will never be able to succeed in anything that you do if you harbor those types of feelings. Let that toxic friend go because it is not worth the heartaches or health problems that can occur from it.

If you aren't a strong-willed person, then you may have encountered that friend who would hurt you by suggesting you smoke, drink, do drugs, and be promiscuous. Peer pressure can be toxic to you. You will drink until you are falling out drunk, smoke until you get high, and have sex with everyone who shows you attention. If your friend feels that partying is the only way to have a good time, or wearing suggestive clothing is the only way to get attention, then this friend is a toxic friend. They are hurting you by allowing you to hurt yourself and do things that show no self-respect.

You are hurting yourself and your body when you do these things. You probably don't realize that the things you do to your body when you are young will affect your body when you are old. Take care of your temple; it's the only one you have. Friends don't let friends hurt themselves in the name of having a good time, just like friends don't let friends drink and drive.

If you have friends who are constantly beating you up and causing you pain physically and emotionally, then they are toxic. We make excuses for their actions and believe that it was only one time and it won't happen again. No one should ever put their hands on you. If it happened once, it will happen again. If your friend is beating you up, make sure you speak up and ask for help. Help is available for people who are abused. Speak up before it's too late and take all the necessary steps to get out of the abusive relationship.

If a friend verbally abuses you by calling you names other than what your birth name is, then they are a toxic friend. I am talking about the adjectives that describe you in the worst way. Friends who tell you that you are a nobody; that no one likes you; and call you fat, ugly, stupid, and thin are toxic. If your friends call you names to make you feel bad about yourself, they are not your friends.

I remember when people who I thought were my friends called me "Big Head." I used to hate being called such. I remember getting in fights as a child because of the name-calling. I would go home, cry, and sit in my room alone. I used to look at my head and wonder why it was big. I realized that my big head was what made me unique. Once I became an adult, I embraced my "big head" and my natural beauty that I carried on the inside and out. It didn't bother me anymore because I became comfortable with who I was and what I looked like. It was even worse when I was called names by other people and my friends laughed.

Have you ever had friends who were bigger than you who always called you too skinny? I hated that. I had several friends who always made fun of me because I was smaller than them. They would call me names and tell me how skinny I was. I always wanted to tell them that they were fat, but I never was the type to hurt anyone's feelings.

Being called too fat or too skinny is hurtful on both sides. Larger friends don't realize that skinny friends don't like to be called names. Sometimes suggestions would be made saying they need to eat more. People who make fun of others' weight are extremely jealous and unhappy with their own weight. If you gained a few pounds, friends who were bigger than you would always notice and tell you that you gained weight. I remember looking at my friends who said this to me and telling them that it looked like they didn't lose any weight. This would shut them up and make them think twice before calling me names again. It wasn't until I became an adult that I realized that my larger friends were jealous of my weight. Behind closed doors, they would exercise and try to be skinny like me.

Friends who call friends names are toxic friends. This type of friend does this to empower themselves, make themselves feel good, and make you feel bad. They are usually unhappy with their lives and want to make sure you are unhappy with yours.

Have you ever had a friend who never compliments you, but you always gave your friend compliments? It seems strange that I asked that question, but this happens. Some friends don't want you to look better than them. If you have good looks, a nice shape, and you dress nice or have it going on, there will always be a problem, if you have a toxic friend. Everything revolves around them, so they get intimidated by you being you. A toxic friend will never compliment you because they are jealous and unhappy with who they are.

On the flip side of friends who say they will never hurt you, you will have that *friend who likes to see you hurt.* They will chuckle inside at the very sight of your pain. They will show concern, but deep down, they are saying "good for you." Yes, people are cruel. They have a warped way of thinking, especially if they are a toxic friend. Some people thrive on seeing others hurt and in pain. Recognize the signs. Evaluate your friendship, and when you see the signs, move on.

I am jealous of you . . . and envious too. We all have experienced that friend who is jealous and envious. Let me explain the difference between the two. A jealous friend will not be happy for you when you achieve certain goals in life. They wish it was them and not you. An envious friend will have the same things, but don't want you to have or achieve the same things they have. It's okay for your friend to have the better things in life, but it's not okay for you to have the same. A jealous and envious friend is a deceitful friend who should be considered toxic. This type of friend is sometimes the more difficult one to determine because of the deceit that comes with it. You would have to really pay close attention to this friend. They will smile in your face and curse you behind your back.

This type of friend is a good actor. They will appear to be happy at all times. Behind closed doors, they will show their true colors. I would rather have a friend who always tells it like it is, whether I like it or not. This is a true friend. This type of friend usually isn't the jealous type. They can be brutally honest. You want that in a friend. If your friend always agrees with you in everything that you do, then there's a chance that they want you to fail and they are jealous of you.

I had a friend whose family supported her and provided all her needs. She was the only one who was driving; she had her own car, an apartment, and a career. She got very upset because I got an apartment and started a business. She tried to discourage me by telling me that my new business was not a good one and that it would not succeed. I knew that I was stepping out on faith when I decided to start my business.

I always had the entrepreneur mind-set, but I needed to financially be able to do it. I went to my friend to get her input. Some things that I said to her, I knew were crazy ideas. She didn't challenge anything that I said to her. She wasn't engaged in any of the conversation. The only thing she said to me was that I shouldn't start a business. She never gave me a reason why.

After weeks went by, I started noticing that she would *roll her eyes* at me every time I crossed a hurdle in my business venture. It was killing her inside knowing that I was about to have my own business. She liked it better when it was her who had it going on. Both of us couldn't have it going on . . . together.

My friend was a toxic friend. I got rid of her.

Since we are speaking about businesses, how many of you have that friend who *tells all of your business?* If you haven't experienced that yet, then good for you! Toxic friends will tell others your business as soon as you turn your back. We are always sharing too much information, whether it's with our friends or on social media. Social media can be toxic too, but that's a separate book.

First, we need to learn to keep our business to ourselves. In a perfect world, that would be the case. If you have a friend who is your best friend, you will share almost everything with them. You are under the assumption that your friendship will last forever and ever. How many of you have realized that you were wrong? If you have that one friend who is a true one, please hold on to them and don't take their friendship for granted. True friends are hard to find. Toxic ones are easy to come by.

Some friendships start during childhood. You will do things with your friend that you expect to take to your grave . . . Not to mention, if they see you climbing the ladder of success, they will find a way to make sure your business gets out. They will do anything to discredit you. Stop giving your friends ammunition to use against you by telling them all of your business. A true friend will keep it to themselves while a toxic friend will share it.

Have you ever noticed regular people who became celebrities and, all of a sudden, everything they did in their past resurfaced to discredit their success? Some of the negative press helped some celebrities gain more stardom, while other negative press blackballed stars in the business for years. Eventually, people tend to forget, and they get back on top again. The more success you have, the more problems you encounter.

Let go of that toxic friend. They will do all they can to hurt you because they are self-centered, jealous, and envious of you.

Chapter 6

Friends who are liars are the type of friends who are deceitful and toxic. If you can't believe anything they say, then why keep them as a friend? Have you had a friend who would lie about the color of the sky? You know that the sky is blue, but they will tell you that the sky is green. If you have a friend who lies all the time, they are really trying to impress you. They are usually unhappy with their lives, so they make up an imaginary one.

I have had friends who would lie about every aspect of their lives. Have you had that friend who would make you feel like they have it going on, but they don't? Social media is the perfect example of friends who lie. Friends will usually lie on social media because they believe, from other friends' posts, that they are doing well. So they try to compete to make it appear that they are doing well also.

Friends who lie all the time will likely steal too. Have you ever had items go missing when your friend was around? When you go to question them about the item, they say they don't have it—but months later, it happens to turn back up when your friend comes around again. They will say they borrowed it, which is fine, but they never let you know they had it. If you have to constantly research everything that your friend tells you, then they are a toxic friend. One day the lies that your friend tells you will catch up with him/her, and you may be caught up in drama that you have no control over. Be careful because this type of friend will have you caught up behind bars.

I knew this teenage girl named Rosas who was a track star. She was a colleague's daughter. Rosas and her friends were all track stars. After their track meet, they would always hang out. One day, the three of them were supposed to meet up to go hang out. One of the friends asked Rosas if she could pick the others up. Rosas asked why they could not drive, and the girl lied and said her car was broke. Rosas agreed to do it. When she arrived at the house, the girls asked her to take them to another girl's house so that they could get their books for school. Rosas took the girls to the house, and they asked her to wait in the car. She waited, and ten minutes later, the girls ran out of the house and told her to drive off fast. The girls robbed a home! Rosas did not know that she was an accessory to a robbery! Rosas tried to fit in with her friends and did not know how to discern whether they were people whom she should hang out with. In school, teenagers care about being popular. They want to be liked by their friends.

As I said before, friends who lie to you will steal. All the girls were apprehended by the police and were transported to the juvenile detention center. Rosas had toxic friends. Her mother warned her about her friends and chastised her often about whom she was hanging out with. Of course, as a teenager, you don't listen to your parents. Not listening did cost her her freedom. A toxic friend will lie about everything. They will lie about their family, friends, job, career, and anything that is worth lying about. They only do this to make themselves look good.

Friends who lie often are the same friends who will *speak negatively about you* to others—or perhaps I should make it plain and say that they will talk about you behind your back. Be careful of this type of friend. If people are telling you that your friend is saying things about you, believe it. There is always some truth to it. I dislike the type of friend who does this to you. We already know that this friend will lie, so why won't they talk about you behind your back? This is a toxic friend. We wouldn't know that this friend is doing this unless you hear them or someone lets you know. Think of all the times you spent with your friend in your face, laughing and having a great time, sharing intimate thoughts and feelings; then you find out that those same things that you shared, your friend used it against you.

A toxic friend will tell all of your business and talk about you. Previously, I warned you about sharing too much information with your friends. Most friendships are for seasons and don't last forever. With that said, it brings me to the belief that true friendships will last forever.

We will be friends forever. This statement is one that we all want to believe in when we choose our friends. No one seeks a friendship thinking that it will end. A new friendship begins fresh and exciting. Everyone seems to be on their best behavior in the beginning. Some friendships are for seasons and others are for a reason. This may be your season to experience a toxic friend so that you can learn a lesson.

Have you ever had a friendship that ended abruptly? I had a friend, and I never thought our friendship would end. As I started to grow more in my faith and success, our friendship started to diminish. I would share everything with her and tried to include her in on every aspect of my career. I began to travel more and experience new things. One day, she just excluded herself from my life. I called, texted, and visited her, but she was never available to see me or answer my calls. It was like she dropped off the planet. Hopefully, you will be able to discern what a toxic friend is like at this point. A swift determination will halt any physical or mental problems that can occur when you have a toxic friend. We make mistakes often when we choose our friends, and once we acquire friends, the mistakes grow. It is up to us to recognize it, learn from it, and move on.

Sometimes the signs are visible, but we are so blinded by friendship that we don't see them. Having a toxic friend really hurts you physically, emotionally, and mentally. We expect our friendships to last. Do you really want it to last now that you know it is toxic? No one does. Are you the toxic friend?

They always complain about everything and can never find anything positive to say. If you are happy, they will find a way to bring your happy spirit down. They don't seem to like being happy. A miserable friend doesn't want to be alone. They need company so they won't be alone in their self-loathing. Surround yourself with positive people, not miserable ones. Negative energy is toxic.

I was a happy individual until my experiences changed the way I felt about things. I had to search my soul and change my thoughts so I could be happy again. Even with my dismay, I always hid my true feelings so no one knew what was really going on with me. I kept a smile on my face and tried to stay positive. I always would feel others' energy, and I could tell almost immediately if it was negative and draining. I didn't like being around people who drained my energy. I didn't want to be the person who had negative energy.

As I started writing this book, I had all intentions on it being a book for everybody to read. I felt like it would be relatable because everyone has experienced a toxic relationship at some point in their life. I couldn't end it without speaking to the ladies about the *toxic man*. I know I struck a nerve because you are looking at your man now, wondering if he is toxic. Ask yourself this question: Does your man only see you for a few hours at night? If your man sees you in the night hours only, you need to ask yourself if he really is your man. He obviously does not want anyone to know you exist. It's even worse if he only sees you in a hotel or at *your* place. If your man does not take you out in public, then he isn't your man. He is hiding you from the world. He has secrets that he wants to be kept in the dark. We always try to find love in the wrong places. We also don't realize that we are in a toxic relationship when it comes to our man. Love can sometimes blind us from what we truly need to see.

Does your man always make promises that he does not keep? Oh yes, a toxic one does. He may promise you the world. He may tell you that he will wine and dine you. The promises that he makes keeps you holding on. You have restless nights just thinking about what he promises to do for you. As you know by now, broken promises will break your heart.

How many of your hearts have been broken? A toxic man will be smooth with his words. He will say anything to keep you holding on. If your man does more talking than doing, then he is toxic. He is constantly breaking your heart. If there is no substance in his promises, let him go. Has your man promised to marry you, but it's been five years and he hasn't proposed? If you think he is going to marry you after courting you that long, then you need to rethink your relationship. He is content with the way things are and likes having his freedom at the same time. Why should he marry you when he is reaping all the benefits of being in a relationship with you so long? Why should he mess up a good thing? He is committed to you, but as soon as something better comes along, he won't have to worry about leaving with baggage.

It can be stressful for a woman who wants to get married, but the man she loves doesn't want to. A woman will hold on for years, with a hope and a prayer. I am not saying that hoping and praying won't change things, but we have to be vigilant in reading the signs and discerning for ourselves what is good for us and what is not. A toxic man will have you emotionally crazy. You will find yourself doing things that are out of character.

Do you find yourself constantly wanting to see him, calling him every hour of the day, checking his cell phone, following him, questioning him, and accusing him of things? These are signs that you do not trust him. If you do this, then *you* are toxic to him because you are stalking him; and he is toxic to you because the relationship is driving you crazy. Unless you can figure out what will make the relationship a healthy one, where you can communicate and compromise, then it is not worth the heartache and pain. Let it go.

Chapter 7

The day I realized that I was a toxic friend occurred when I looked in the mirror. I saw a woman scorned and emotionally abused by relationships that changed the way I viewed people and my friendships. I lied to myself and believed that I had forgiven all those who had caused me heartache and pain, when the truth is, I have not. My smile concealed certain emotions. My eyes were not misleading, as you could see my spirit was broken. I used to say that you must forgive and forget, but I did not practice what I preached. I contemplated ways to overcome the pain by creating pain for the people whom I considered were toxic friends. I wanted them to feel what I felt. I wanted them to understand that what goes around comes around.

If my friend said something that hurt me, I would say something to hurt them in return. I had a way with words. I knew which ones to use that would strike a nerve. Remember the childhood saying, "Sticks and stones will break my bones, but words will never hurt me"? Truth is, words do hurt people. Sometimes, my reaction time wasn't quick, so the hurtful words would marinate inside me. Hiding my thoughts was toxic for me. It made me angry and resentful.

If my friend wasn't there for me, I would find a way to make myself unavailable. When my friend called me, I would not answer the telephone, or I would let them call repeatedly until I was ready to speak again. I wanted the experience to be mutual. I did hurtful things myself that made me toxic.

Looking back, I understood why my friend didn't return my calls. As my resentment grew, I became more toxic. I wasn't likable. My energy was draining, and I wasn't a pleasure to be around. I was so hurt that I became the person that I did not want to be. I didn't know that I was.

Accepting that I was a toxic friend was very difficult for me. I found fault with others but did not see it within myself. I wanted to believe that I was the *perfect friend,* when I wasn't. I responded to my friends' actions, by reciprocating it to them. I am sure that I caused my friends the same emotional pain they have caused me. This was wrong. It didn't make me a better person. I missed many blessings in my life because of this. I remember chuckling inside when I felt like *I got them back.* In the end, I didn't get them back. I did things on purpose, and very slickly. I chose words that I knew would hurt, and I said things that I knew would get on my friends nerves. I hurt myself even more. It took too much effort and energy to make my friends miserable. Why did I do this? Did I gain anything from it? No, I gained more heartache and pain. All it did was push my friends away from me even more, and our relationship would not have a chance at mending itself.

Many of us have been toxic at one point in our lives. Once you realize that you are, you can change it. Ask yourself what makes you toxic. Are you harboring negative thoughts and feelings toward your friend? Have you forgiven all who have hurt you? Have you moved on? If you can't truthfully answer any of these questions, then you are lying to yourself. We have to look in the mirror and ask ourselves, "What can I do to be a better person?" It is always easier to find fault with someone else, but it is never easy to find fault with yourself.

When my friends turned into enemies, I asked myself why. What did I do? I know what they did, but what did I do to change things? I looked in the mirror. I realized that I was a toxic friend. Of course, I did not want to accept it, and it actually was difficult to admit. With time, I learned that I was just as guilty as my friend. I understood what it meant to be toxic. I don't like being a toxic friend. I want to be a supportive friend who unconditionally loves and forgives. I want to be that friend you can count on during difficult times. I want to celebrate success and encourage during failures. I want to laugh during the good times and be the shoulder to cry on during the bad times.

I am now the type of friend who uplifts, encourages, motivates, and promotes others to be the best that they can be. I can admit I wasn't always this way. I celebrated many, but I didn't if I felt like I was hurt by someone. It was the day I looked in the mirror at myself, *realizing the one finger that I pointed at my friend left four fingers pointing back at me.* I prayed, searched my heart, and cried for many days. I realized the mistakes I had made over the years. We are all entitled to make mistakes that we learn from. This is one of the beauties of life. We live and we learn.

I have learned a lot about people over the years. I have shared my experiences with you—not only for you to understand how to discern toxic friends, but to see if you are one too.

Chapter 8

Fake friends. Throughout this book, I have been focused on toxic friends. Honestly, a *toxic friend is a fake friend.* How many of you have fake friends? Several times, I have mentioned an example of a fake friend. You didn't need an example, because as soon as you read the title "fake friend," you immediately could name a few. Why is this friend in your life? Are you the fake friend?

I can answer the question why we keep this type of friend in our lives. We do because we don't realize how toxic the relationship is. You don't realize that *you* are the toxic friend. We keep these people in our lives because they have always been there. They may have been there since grade school. We don't understand that there is a season for everyone and everything. Just because you have known someone for years doesn't mean they have to be a part of your life forever. Friends come and go. Only the friends that are supposed to be there will be. It is part of the process and your growth.

We have to go through the process of elimination. No one said the process would be easy. No one said it wouldn't affect your heart. I feel as if we all have to experience having a fake friend so when the real one comes, we will appreciate them.

What is a fake friend? A fake friend is one who deceives you into believing that they are a true friend to you. A fake friend will act like they are happy for you. They will never be there for you, talk about you to others behind your back, receive but never give, disrespect you, hurt you, discourage you, lie, cheat, steal, be envious and jealous, beat you up, and they will leave you. A fake friend does not want to see you happy or successful. They will, however, play the part of a true friend so that they can reap the benefits of having you in their life.

A fake friend can be an opportunist. They will call you from time to time, check up on you, and keep you around because of what you can do for them. They know how beneficial it is to have you. A fake friend will use you as long as you let them. They are like vampires who suck your blood dry. A fake friend will attempt to kill your dreams and your spirit. It goes back to sharing too much information to your friend. You may ask a friend to pray for you. They may say a prayer, but not the prayer you need. They may pray that you fail. They may pray for failure, but *no weapon that formed against you shall prosper.* Sometimes intentions aren't clear, but if you ask for discernment, it will be shown to you. At some point in your life, you have experienced a fake friend. They are easy to come by but hard to get rid of. If you see the signs of a fake friend, run before they become toxic. If you are the fake friend, it's time to accept it and decide to make a change.

Every season in our lives, we encounter people who are there for a reason. Even though some people are fake, we always learn a lesson from each encounter. Some lessons are difficult to digest, but it helps us grow to become better people in all aspects of our lives. The lessons we learn are testimonies we can share with others to help them grow. People don't like sharing testimonies with others because of the fear of being judged. Everyone has a story. Your story is a testimony. It can help others who are struggling and don't have anywhere to turn. Testimonies let people see that everyone is human and makes mistakes. I know I have made more mistakes than I can count. I don't care what people think. I know that I have suffered for many years, and I am still standing. I know that I am destined to share my experiences with others to help them. I know that you have to *go through to get through*. Being judgmental is toxic and it only stops your blessings, and it can cause you to go through the exact thing that you judge. You need to be very careful, because I do believe there is power in the tongue.

I won't focus on fake friends anymore. I want to focus on *you*. We already established that toxic and fake friends are the same. We also know that we have to look at ourselves in the mirror to decide what type of friend we are. Did you look in the mirror? Look deep into your eyes then close your eyes. Ask yourself, "Who am I? Am I who I say I am? Am I true to myself? Am I toxic?" Now open your eyes. If you really searched within your soul, your eyes should have a tear trying to release.

It's okay to release it. It's okay to cry. Crying is good for the soul. It cleanses the soul. It just shows that you honestly feel that you need to work on *you*. As I am writing these words, tears start to form in my eyes. My heart started to beat fast with anxiety. I struck a nerve within myself. I feel as if everything I am saying is a confirmation that we all need to improve. I feel that this book will help people search their souls as I have.

When I looked in the mirror, I asked myself what I can do to change. I cried as I opened my eyes after I asked myself the same questions that I asked you. I knew I had a lot of work to do to be a better me. There were five things I needed to do. I needed to accept, forgive, love, change, and move on. As I looked back on my relationships, I realized I needed to *accept* responsibility for failed relationships. Sometimes, your ego will make it difficult to accept responsibility when you feel that you did nothing wrong. Acceptance will allow you to open the doors to self-improvement. I disliked who I became—a person who harbored hate and resentment in my heart.

Hate is a powerful word. I don't like using it, but in this case, I have to. I hated who I was. I hated my friends only because they did not show concern toward me, my well-being, and my world. I had to change within myself, but it was not easy. Being able to accept indicates growth. Growing isn't always easy. We may stumble and fall many times. It's okay, because it's all part of the process.

I understand that many of you are probably saying that your friend needs to accept that they did you wrong. Don't worry about whether they accept it or not. It's not your battle. It is their battle. When it's their season to accept their wrongdoings and how they treat people, that's their business. All you have to do is worry about you. Remember, there is a season for everyone.

Once you have accepted that you have to work on yourself, you need to ask for *forgiveness* from God and forgive those who hurt you. Forgiveness is a powerful tool, and it should not be taken lightly. If you are a spiritual being, you will understand how important it is to forgive.

Things happen in your life for a reason. We have to learn from the situations that we encounter. As great as we think we are, there is still room to grow into a better person. No one is perfect. Sometimes we have to accept the things that we can't change. Love people for who they are and not what you want them to be.

I had to do this. I needed to accept that God made each and every human being to be unique. We all have faults. We can't force anyone to change who they are to satisfy our needs. Yes, they did you wrong, but two wrongs don't make it right. If you forgive, you will be able to *love* unconditionally, even if someone did wrong by you. Try to *change* to be a better person and *move on* so you can receive the blessings that are in your future. Stop holding on to the past. The way you view your past will hinder you from moving forward in your future. Time will heal a broken heart, but working to change your mind-set will heal the heart swiftly. Don't let the past dictate your future. We have to live in the present and embrace our faith, while having hope in our future.

Once you have worked on yourself, *true friends will come.* Your energy will attract your heart's desires. You will attract like-minded people who will support and be true to you in everything you do. You will be able to understand and reciprocate the true values of having a friend. You will be able to connect with people who will motivate, encourage, and uplift you during your journey to self-improvement and success.

When you are blessed with a true friend, you will have to constantly work on yourself so you won't become a toxic friend. A true friend shows happiness when you succeed in obtaining your heart's desires. They will keep it real while encouraging you. They will be there for you in your time of need to uplift you, be truthful, and to create positive energy while the friendship thrives.

Cherish your friendships. Keep them close to your heart and watch the fruits of a beautiful friendship flourish into a lifetime of memories.

About The Author

Joyce M. Gilliard is an emerging author. This is Joyce's first book. She has always had a passion for writing since childhood and decided to step out on faith to make her passion a reality. She is a wife, mother, and hairstylist in the film industry. She is a motivational speaker who encourages others to pursue their dreams and live their life to the fullest. She has completed several books and will be publishing them in the future.

Edwards Brothers Malloy
Thorofare, NJ USA
April 1, 2016